Fab

BY THE SAME AUTHOR

POETRY

Wao

Fab

by

PAUL BLOUNT

THE CLUNY PRESS
ST. ASAPH
2009

First published in 2009 by

The Cluny Press
Eirianfa
The Roe
St. Asaph
Denbighshire LL17 0LU
Wales

Copyright © Paul Blount, 2009

The right of Paul Blount to be identified as author
of this work has been asserted in accordance with Section 77
of the Copyright, Designs and Patents Act 1988

A CIP catalogue record for this book is available from the British Library

ISBN 978–0–9547610–1–1

Typeset by Discript Limited, London WC2N 4BN
Printed in England by Good News Press

for my parents who gave me life
and Chris Ogden
and the robot called da Vinci who saved my life

there is no contradiction between
love and discipline

Daniel Barenboim, Reith Lecture

Contents

Ribbons

I have ribbons for your hair,
I have streamed them from the river,
tied them to the clouds.
Their colours are different, one from one,
me from you,
you from me and others.

I have ribbons from the river
for your hair. Clear, clean, cleansing
close light for your hair,
from the river, streaming.

I have river for your hair,
river is thorough, heavy, slow.
River is mad, moving, like wind moves hair.
I have ribbons for your hair.

May I Presume to Walk With You?

May I presume to walk with you?
Alone as I find you here
owl scored
called.
Escort the steps you take,
be an escort to your beauty.

Along the narrow alley way,
protect the sun slant shadow
triangle upon a plastered gaze
blaze, glaze biscuit wall.
Assume,
walk by your side
shadow into the triangle
and you.

May I presume to walk with you?
And by your side offer hand for hand guide the steps you take:
and hold time independent swing of movement
hand in hand,
mouth in mouth,
eye in eye,
a mad, blind, stumbling, alley-drunk thing.

May I presume to walk with you?
And sing.

Tenandry

You are a soft spray salt sea tear, a scent
ocean beating deep within me.
All the oceans of the world.
Sea witch curse me,
command the ocean rage storm against me.
Sea witch rend me. Issue fire.
Rape your touch on me,
craze innocence, leaf brown, green.
You are a dark secret place
known only to me.
Where the wind is born,
all the winds that blow across the sea.
You are spring green beauty, blowing over me.

On the Moor

My dream is to walk on the moor when light
defines the air,
as seen when the hill is in grey
and the mist hangs, falls and envelopes all there.
To feel, at first, the damp
and then the sharp bite
and rush of uncertainty, as colours become
as when sky is blue,
moss, green and pale
and the deer are russet in your hair
and a flower breathes against your face
and I delight in the joy in your eyes.

Hallowe'en

Colour sleet falls.
As if a white starched pillow was opened
having been pressed in tissue paper leaves,
shaken out, to air.
Caught on a wind from the west:
from Moidart, where the early spring's buds
are dying now.

A paintbox falls from the west,
as if time had come to drain the world.
The sky is dark, grey-blue.

Thrown colour wind from the west,
wood shaven-scented, check fleeced.
Glowing, light ablaze in a kiln,
washing a year's ideas.

Red tears on grass.

When You Arrived

When you arrived
I had planned to bathe you in scented herbs,
in a vat of meadowsweet and woodruff.
I had planned to blow the leaves from the grass

from the dying tree.
And when bathed, I was to dry you
in a warm lavender towel from head to toe,
thoroughly.

And carry you to flowers wild
of mixed fortune and shade,
upon Lady's bedstraw and lovage
and lay with you in leaf, herb, flower
and warm, warm scent
in your hair, lips, breasts and thighs
and me.

And, if presentable, I was to ask my lady,
"May I come to the herbs and flowers
and smell the sea in your hair,
and with my body the musk of your femininity?"

But my lady did not come,
though she had said, "No, not drown, I shall come."
The leaf and the dying tree.

Thirty Odd Years Ago

When I was planted, thirty odd years ago, and from when I
grew, I
grew tall and straight and enjoyed company:
the summer swallows who circled my canopy
and I enjoyed hope:
the feeling that requirements set at seed had been met
I felt I was how a tree should look.

For thirty, odd, years I undressed for the winter –
warmth beneath the snow with you
and for thirty years in summers high and summers low
I dressed for the evening
and your privilege.

And when my strength was pure, and I knew it at thirty four
why then did you bring the smell of diesel to me
and the burn taste saw-powered blade within the circle of my
ring and increase the temperature of
wood fire in my veins.

You had made me fixed
had stationed me with nature, thrown on a potter's wheel
I had clay and water.

Cherry Blossom Tree

The cherry blossom tree is showering confetti today.
Showering spring,
landscaping.
Showering spring with cherry tinted leaves
in a renewed vow of love.

Spring

Did you run here from there with
wind and rainbow and blowing in your
hair? Making blow back hair blow
back. Crossing heads with the sky in mind.

Skulls shaking all the four ways there are.
Across, back, forward, down, up.
Beside. Many more than four.
People
to contemplate shaking off.
Running with reason in the legs.
Running without reason in the heart
or, heart legs confused by running.
Shaking hair in the air in the sun
for the
first time, this year.

The First Time I Saw Your Face

the rise
the even
the evening fall
covered in fur,
stone-age prices,
red opening
red meets red
covered in fur
repeat, repeat
repeat
retreat
the musk,
male
musk-deer

lines drawn on hand made paper
creased, closed
posted

stamped

Locked

I am to build a dry stane dyke.
High.

I wish the running squeal of laughter
Held head high.

Fast.

Your head,
Rushing spring into summer.

Us.

Locked.

Ring Fort

I will roll boulders into a ring
forty feet thick, an acre wide.
The ring will be mine
and you will be encircled in the ring
and with boulders and wood
we will build love.

Poplar

When I prayed to the alight tree at night,
with love reflected in the river, with certainty.
Why doubt the reflections?
Why does it seem the other way round
in a mirror?

When I worried about tomorrow,
about the purchasing power of sterling against the dollar
and tomorrow's purchase of the tree, the river,
love
your beauty.

Foolish, isn't it, prayers,
praying before a poplar tree?
So many children for the alight tree to support,
bees for nectar
and moths for comfort.

Keltneyburn

Keltnyburn water curves right, to the left
fall curve timbre, right to left;
dash of colour caresses
the curve of your cheek.
Rudd coloured cheek.

The promise made to a juvenile pike
at the taking of his first roach.
Above, butterflies fly in, fly out,
fly-drown into the moth fall.

For Another

Between three a.m. and sixty three apple green years
of cool half-line sleep,
watching your
otter paw hand soft nested between legs
and sucking thumb foetally mouthed
hind
hide
hidden
leaning into Hind.
Curled, tied into the earth.

Tectonics. Earth slip.
Finger loosening grip, curled fingers parting
pawing at teat.
Buck at teat, hampering young gander
drinking sixty three throat chocked, closed years dry.
Bush dry.
After-birth dry.

Ecuador

The fire is in Ecuador.
Forest fire from your eyes,
in rainbow birdwing butterfly, iridescent
violet in your hair.
In the Amazon, Ecuador, Peru, Korea.
Who knows how strong the wing beats?
Red
Indigo
Violet
Blue
Yellow.

Arizona Plane

Arizona plane,
plain sand grains desert dry.
Tee-shirt white.
Vest parched, sun spot dried bone,
blanched,
made white.

Water meadow, cedar wood red,
averts the day when drooped head
bays became green in an old man's
pleasure mind.
Turns the herring bone brain.

Larched polished, waxed,
varnished mask.

Balnagard Burn

Watching it you cannot describe it.
Waterfall,
until, beside it
it describes you.

Juniper thicket hum in the pour
sheer power surety
of glacier deer veined remnant fall.
Prickle and barb,
gin clear rocks distilled from ice.

Dawn hit raid.
Strike force.
Revolution.

Vermont in the Fall,
round up time.

Autumn Full Moon

Kicked in mis-shapen moon, big as a dew pond.
No currents, plenty of scars.
Fills up once a month.
Covered by clouds for skaters to dance on,
twist and turn and serrate on edge
on monthly trips from the stars.

Holds many skaters
fallen through
drowned.

No beat has ever been recorded back.
Absorbs shock.
Gives way, sucks away.
Sucks in, in, in.

Suck, my moon, and never release,
Always cool and non-dependent of my stare.
Take the skaters from the stars.
I shall come and be yours.

And I to Taste

And I to taste your heather honey hair
dry, breathe dry, the nectar-damp behind your ear
and the necklace lava, flowing, curving
round the blush of your cheek
and into your mouth.
My mouth promised a heather honey, snow coloured,
waterfall pool,
where I would play the bat right through
red to the covers, ground high.

George Mackay Brown

George Mackay Brown circled his country girl seven times.
I have four points to my round.
The first, the north, is to the north, the dark, cold
disquiet of unsure; sea-shore unquiet.
The second, the east, is the hold of the glowing owl
on the slow worm.
The third, the south, is to the summer shieling,
full song.
Full of milk from a mad cow.
The fourth, the west, is to the south-west wind,
fresh,
breathing your scent
sun kiss quick
slowing your caress.

I tie my circle around your beauty
and ask,
"What is there to forgive, ever?"

Domino Pub

He carried her look like a leaf
on the wind
like the sea crest lap,
white
lick lap top lick, top crest
look.
Sea proud, pounding
poundage, Plimsoll line,
money and the mockery of man.

When laughter at the bar is Irish
and her look wondrous and joyous.
April, swifts in the evening.

I See Chlorophyll Is With Us Again

I see the poplar is with us again,
arrived the same time as usual.
End of May. Always late.
The last to arrive at the party
for cocktails at eight.
Summer time.

I see the stone-age birds are with us again.
A bit late. Later than last year.
They never seem to improve their technology.
Their time seems all awry.

I see the bats are not with us again.
Winter damage? Or, bad hosts?
Or, perhaps, after a surreal experience
on the Stock Exchange, they went bust.

I see chlorophyll is with us again.
Incidentally, a still mouse is smiling
forever on a stone by the waterfall,
the colours silt to chocolate blancmange.

When You Are No Longer There

And when I catch your breath
I cry with fright at what my grief will be
when you are no longer there
to breathe my love
and May is blown out for the last time.

Or if it first be me
then I bequeath my body
to the hawking, garrotting gull
and my soul to you,
compass true.

Mother, Daughter

It's all in the angle of the stance,
in the stance movement.
The jerk, re-angled positions
to the pore.
Scented in memory through the stance.
It's all in the vixen licking her cub,
underneath and across her hair.
Between her legs, correcting her form,
defining her stance.
Clearing her eyes with her tongue,
drying her stare on her fur.

Lambing Season

When a lamb is born he wants his mother.
He milks her motherliness, mouthes his
need around her shape.

The two of their sex sleep like alligators in a creek.

Sheep gad about singing nursery rhymes

of hope and promise,
and the infusion of confidence
of being bold.

The lambs, before they consider bookselling as a career,
fit their lives around the tails of others
and watch doves planning their flights
of great fancy.

The lambs then self destruct.

Standing on the Shore

I perceive a figure standing on the shore
arm raised straight, to point the gull
and the sperm bank sea.

Mop, flower wild head, all eyes,
giggling at power's rudeness.

The sea's very maleness washing her ankles,
then swimming its salt over her
as she feels authority,
enjoying her line through the power, push, pull
slow stone liquidiser, sky line strength.

No, he will not stop now
for White-letter hairstreaks banned from the land.

Miners' Strike

During a yellow sun hot afternoon
I placed my arm into a well
and ran my hand along the cool
coal seam
and thought of breaking the seam
for the sun to yellow
and of alchemy:
to turn the black into gold.

The Fear of Death in a Child

The fool is in his lair, grumpy.
Crest-fallen-long.
Drooping.
Pinch
jester's hat
on which hangs a bell.
Off tune.
Flat.
Contemplating unconditional love;
conditional love.

boy,
eleven winters weak, about to die.
Says: "It's not like death
because death is losing a good body.
My body has always been dead. So, I am
leaving death;
a dead thing.
What's left of me will be spirit
which, Angels be, will return
and be a good Angel to others,
to you all."

Attitude problems, with parents, and others.
At eleven: response to fear.
The fear of Grown-Up sweat,
on their faces
and then,
on my face.

Classical thoughts.
Classics, never learnt.
Classical music,
never heard: Eva Turner.
Forget yesterday, live for today,
no tomorrow
response.

Tuning fork wrong.

She

Head held peered low
children adultly shoal to school
surveying the adult world
adroitly wrapping around adult cracks
parting pavements.
Adults in the gutter.

The Pakistani stroked by his heart
thirty three philosophically fills his lungs
with vodka, ice
and a splash of lemonade.

Lemonade, crisps and
Irn Bru shape the satchel
on their backs.

One in the shoal,
toddler, red
sixties outfit.
Mother, Greenham
ethnic outfit.
Man, hair, beard,
grabbing gobbled ice
at the bar
is accompanied by his parents.

They to meditation class
for stress and tension and the company
of *Guardian* readers.

She
eventually to read
She.

Appeal to Maggie

Appeal to Maggie.
Maggie Bella make them come, come.
Make them dry. Make them come.
Maggie.
Maggie Bella. You know.
Give your blessing.
Do not go.
Be with us, always.

Nothing can stand between my love and I.
To blow sweet into your air.
Allow me to warm your tear
and blow soft
"Swing low, sweet chariot."

Exhilarate your countenance.
Show I am not male.

Tench

Word
words that can be broken
split apart
like rocks by frost.
Words that can enter a woman's body
seeded,
then sun and fire.

Man cannot be entered, or so one is told.
A frost moon, spirit coloured evening.
Pool.
Chatter, chatter, chatter.

If there is ice, it will be at one place
on the pool, one point where the tench lie.

Thawing, floes forming break the drift.
All that is not man remorselessly goes on.
Chatter, chatter, chatter of water against floe.
Warm air hits the floe, bounces, absorbs:
ice sings the requiem.

South-east, four, continuous slight rain.
Two miles. Falling slowly.
Calm, haze, one mile. Falling more slowly.

Russian dolls. Dawn.
At the pool, morning.
Pebbles deep. Polished, pebbled deep pool
like dream transparent sleep pools,
where, at the time of the moon light ,
a girl swims.

Tench deep turning a bream roll.
Tench beat. Regular.
I wade, cool moon, dawn morning light,
tench moving deep. Spirit surround.
Doctor fish. Spirit healers.
It is said other fish caress
and ailments are no more.

Hand under the frost bellied tench,
frost that holds the dawn.
Not hoar, but inside out, outside in.
Waiting, spirit mist doubtful,
undercurrent swirl, head turned
and again turned head in a bream roll.
Clenched. Tenched clenched.
Slime bite. Hit. Tail.
Eye
dire in swirl.
Heads swirl. Tench, mine
into the whirlpool.
Chatter, chatter, chatter.

Body pulses moon red.
Grammar cracking. Words more distant now.
Enters in to control and be,
to play piano and grow.
Vigilant.
Watching the mother, safe and watching.
Russian dolls,
entered by the second daughter.
Chatter, chatter, chatter.

Withold the sentence.
She is within me now, in cloisters
and singing ice.
Sing songs and sleep.
The dawn is in me.
Unstitching the stitches.

Moon compassion show release,
net free. Let her go, church free.

Thaw clouds over the ice. First white
then grey, upward to crimson into
blue and the tench brown sky.

The birth cry of all that is not man
remorselessly goes on.

The Cerne Abbas Giant

The Cerne Abbas giant roams still the hill
where birth and after-birth stain records
chalk man preparing for the wild hunt and kill.

Sharp first thoughts, bludgeoning rude vanity
re-iterated now on the hill
where hay is gathered in mounds of grandeur
recalling the chalk birth hours,
remembered between her labour and his promises.

That changed inside – thought into colour red:
the camouflage for earth,
that changed outside – thought into colour blue:
the camouflage for sky,
that changed thought into mixed, lying, colours.

The Cerne Abbas giant had laid a thought:
'quark, quark, quark, quark.'
When 'quark' was birth and remembering,
conjuring, playing, leafing, breezing,
juxtaposing before gay time.

The time of winding hedgerow lanes,
courting old oaks.
Fathers and mothers,
mothering soft wooded downs and a feel of air.

The insular, complacent people had not yet come
to father the soldiery and dyke the flaking empire,
rust made hay sour in the lancet mill,
cut rude from the hill.

Cricket Game

Number one
he always played it straight.
Forward. Back. Could read the spinners.
Byzantine was his life: quick and back;
deflect. Soft touch.
Conscious. On-side player. Accumulated fifty.
Got to it.
Out through pace. Beat him. Couldn't believe it.
Given out lbw.

Number two
came in. Hesitant.
Out first ball. Scored a duck.
Blamed the pitch.

She was making the sandwiches.

Smoke Trail

The brown skeleton was unobtrusive.
Two brown sticks held the white cigarette,
kirby-grips held her hair.
She drew on a fat *Capstan* full strength
breath.
There was no shake in her cough,
there was no cough.
She slowly left the cloud
wearing a blue headscarf.

Mother, Father and Son

He was drawn out of her like a weed,
and the root was shaken
to fill the loose rough earth,
and he placed with her
and she pressed her finger against him
for the first time, against her wish
and his father's want.

The root dyes mixed to colour a boy,
that made them painters, sort of artists,
creators.
Like God.
Well, like Mother and Father & Son & Co. Ltd.
A family.
They now were numbers to be counted at Census time.
Pay rates for the family, shop for the family,
push the chair with other mums and dads.
Be responsible and accept a little importance,
bask in their parents' eyes.

She had wanted a Moses baby
to place in his Moses basket.
A baby who would love her,
not a lump of lard,
a baby to gurgle with fullness at the breast.

He had wanted a son for self-admiration,
to emulate exactly, but a touch better,
here and there, this time around.
Just touching up what was already there.

She pressed her finger against him, again,
as she would a wicker basket among the reeds.
Just a few inches from her, to the Nile,
as her baby Moses floated
She pressed her finger against him, for a third time.
Mother instinct press.
Mother nature pressed-flower, as he
tumbled off the edge of the world
into the swirl deep pool darkness
of his fear,
of his ever fall from her touch.

Pulled out of the ground and tossed aside.

Mcgillicuddey's Reeks

He came down the cliff
with Irish mist around his waist,
with plenty of time for making
slow with the hill, to get down.

He clawed down the cliff
and sang the lark sky to see
where the mist had left room
for making steps.

He left the cliff
with a cow tongue hinged in his mouth,
the scent of mist and Ireland.
He never said a word.

Wild and Free

Wild and free,
free and wild,
running in clouds without applause.
Dvořák's String Quartet in F.
When conditions are right I tend to run.

River Tummel

River woke early,
after a slow start and a long learn,
River wanted to know its range.
Ranch boy. Steers.
Cattle range. Tex Ritter. Lone Ranger.
Father, son. Shoot out.

River. Cresta run.
Grown up, relaxed. *Apres-ski,*
enlarging, growing, developing.
Psychologically sound.

River knew it was a late developer
but found sound could ride a stallion,
stallion a wave.
Spray sleep, waking gone, grey remembrance
back to beginnings, rushing back.
Rushing to catch up lost time: a slow developer
released on a country walk at five pm.,
on a Sunday, off the leash, allowed off.

River bolted. Tried what bolted meant.
Tried to define bolting.
Putsch.
A not sound thing witnessed awake, raging,
rearranging unsound, running.

River, ears open, eyes alive, head perched,
stretch, muscle tension gone.
Floating: fast, faster, fastest, free.

Never mind my rage.
Never mind psychology.
Take me to the sea, my break from the cage,
tomorrow I will be recaged.

Tinkers on the Train

Wild young eyes.
Young,
hair wild, along the tunnel in the train,
charging.
Dog on lead,
young, wild eyed, channelled.
Beautiful charge.
Fixed.
Nothing to one side, nothing to the other side.
Three children of the mist,
of the old Gael mist, charge
faster than the train moves.

Dog connected to pram
followed by old woman,
Drunk man and older drunk man.
Pram overladen with blankets for warmth,
the begetting of children
and drink.

Stalin

Stalin
Starling, startling
Sharp
Comb rivulets, channels.
Black. White.
Russian rites.
Chimes
Combing hairs; bees
hair
combs; summer blue
Mischief. Bees rubbing,
hair picking
up
mischief

I clap the wild cat.

Falkland Islands

And I shall go to die.
And I shall go to the sea shore to die.
Bloated, bellied.
Whooper erect.

And I shall go to die.
Whale gorged expanse,
humped flesh.
White might, right, flag-forced flatulence.

And I shall go to die.
Morituri te salutamus.
Salute your ideology
and Alpamayo beauty.

And I shall go to die.
Sea level risen.
Dropped into the foul and fury of twenty thousand feet.
Dropped into the bush of cant.

And I shall go to die.
A bridge of iron screams across the plain
where hyenas dirt play in a pit
fouled by ignorance.

And I shall go to die
where fighting cocks scratch roots from dust ground eyes.
Peck and peck again and peck till red is deep as the sea
with mud.

Better Dead than Red

So, the political system, economic system
are the determinants. Shape mens' lives.
Make life/death decisions for you.
King and Country. Nazi Germany.
Japanese Empires. Vietnamese children
who must understand being napalmed,
and remain South Vietnamese must be
preferable to being over-run by the North Vietnamese.
Eco-political structures are as important as life.

How could I live under the Reds?
Yes, I understand.

Of course, the dawn does not rise at the same time,
the sun no longer shines. Wind, breeze, hay shaken
hair stream into rivers of joy.
And at three in the afternoon in July, say the sixteenth.
The butterflies no longer fly.
Eco-political systems are more important than nature.

After the Demo

She,
right leg crossed over the left leg,
in blue.
Red lips,
belt,
necklace,
black shoes.
Thoughtfully blue for effect.
Transmitting menstruation
drips, mood.
Thoughtfully, slowly, slow.
Red faced,
gold chain,
blue, red.
Black shoes,
on a stool in a bar
dripping the drinks in two hands,
loose.

Creed

How far does the church have to go
before it is realised that
constraints, problems, rules, mores,
constrained or self imposed
pose a question, as it were against itself?

The question is this: the church having lived
through this process,
the process of reduction to nothing,
nothing remains.

What to do?
One answer is as follows, as practiced by many.
When the spit hits the face.
Razor the eyes.
Blind.

Then, mud wash the leaking blood
and stamp with feet and
roll it over
stamping.

Call the result a born again, whatever.

Introduction to a Friend

In September, late
when Autumn swallowed England
and I breathed in Autumn
and climbed the felt covered drey shired dyke,
sat on the back of bits of a ton of horse rock
and into the boyhood lost field.

Lost one cold, crackling, dead, branch-stripped-red
creased November, a generation ago.
When the field was new to me;
no one had set a track,
dreamt a wish,
blown a message,
laid a hand.
My first introduction to a friend
my first chance to revere.
So I dismounted the horse rock
scoffed up the first green snow
and muddied the innocent promise.
Breathed in the smell of treachery, of theft
and stood before the abstract painting.
Breathed in the smell of a fighting drunk man.
Of raw meat.

I was alone.
The field was silent.
The field was treasure.
I laughed at everyone.
The field laughed at everyone.
We were one.

Horse-chestnut trees showered their fruit.
Re-arranged their genes.
A generation later I stole your promise.

Anticipating Autumn

The wood was crinkled red, curly.
Afternoon, red sticks breaking.
Knitting needles clicking the wool,
lashing the dye;
shapes
toadstools
laments.

Red smells smelt,
collected clicks, the needles, the wood,
the stitches

sticking tomorrow's haze,
hazing rising patterns
curly red hair, crinkling

thoughts of you.

The Season's Colour

Salmon, dives, bottoms
below
stranded seams, dead seals. dread nought.
Cruise gravel drag, open cast
Seam. Silent. Still. Discrete. No secrets spoken.
Cruise colour, universe colour
Black
Open black cast, colour cast
Cruise lonely black,
end
The season's colour, the end colour.

Birds' Sky

birds' sky
from telephone lines
data blasts across the sky
communication occurs
facts and figures, directions
small black dots exchange
small back dots, multiply

bird becomes bird exchange
mysterious unheard calls
resonating between the fires

automatic data processing pellets blast the sky to pieces

the earth is forgotten
the year is ended
the sun turns its back

Japan

The trees are waving their handkerchiefs.
Flags fly.
The Shinto chimes, chime the change
of time.
Changing times.
Baroque to relax.
You stiffen.
The trees wave in the fury
of the wind,
to separate fury and relaxation
and tomorrow
what the next minute will bring.
The trees are desperately waving to live.
Japan, do not cut the rain forests
down,
please.

Jisei

Rain
man sheltering under a cherry blossom Fugenzo tree,
as once
he sheltered at his mother's breast,
cradled against her arm.

The Samurai performs *Ikebana.*
Blossom rain arranged to shape
the death-wish ceremony
Seppuku
completes the ritual of the seasons
as the last flower is placed.

Will you carry a torch for me?

Cruise

The sea has a root to the centre of me,
rooted through the earth to appear as trees
linked, unseen; watered
tears and leaves.

Motions lapping the banks of the Nile
where the women wash, wring out stains from clothes.
Sun, sand, sharp, still, stillbirth stains.
Birth stains, growth stains, end stains
wringing through their hands.
Earth mounds, man made big as a wave
heavy as the sea.
Dead sea weight.

Come on, this morning we will violate the sea
and in the afternoon rubbish the earth
with glee.
You and me will be covered under the earth.
Uprooting, over the ground.
Discombining.
You and me.
Hold me.

Abba

"I have to get the Abba sound."
"Yes, I know, love."
"It's really important.
He said he'd get the Abba, just for me."
"Yes, I know, love."
"Can you hear it?"
"Not in the ambulance, love."
"Hold me again."
"I know love, here."

Can you hear it?
Tone, before the owl's stretched disquiet
hold.
Can you feel it?
Cold as the deepest stone,
behind the glass, the menagerie.

Three

Goat, the eye
watching me
that day.
Remembering.
Brown eye, meets me.

Skiers were back in town.
Slush snow, not good
stuff.

Goat was warm, colouring
running yellow, warm.
Yellow. Heat.
Protective, protecting.

Goat was working the hill,
ridge work, pack-drill
speaking.

Three fires coloured the hill.
Links, chains, clamps.
Three ridges chained.
Steel face white.

Goat

Coming from a coward
out of a line of cowards. Given birth with Goatseyes,
married to . . . choosing a fool with no sensitivity.
Having rejected a square concrete playground which reminded
you of you.
Having chosen wild spaces where sheep feed. To lead them.
Yellow eyed. Created, issued, a dead, a coward, another.
Playing formal games with so-called people, so-called friends.
Living a so-called life. Contaminated with sheep disease.
Flocks.
Sheep now yellowed, following.

After the Payment

Picked up a tart. Or more accurately she drew me up.
Screwed left. Screwed right. Screwed me.
She screwed me up, and down. Seaside fashion.
Right and proper. A good professional job.
I was trying to talk to her.
Tell her that Descartes told me the human mind
was basically sound.

Spat me out early in the morning.
After the payment.
After the payment.

London

I've got this theory: we
play the gaming machines atavistically
like the way men and women fuck
away, and every so often
a belt, belt, belt
of reward
the belt, belt, belt of up-front London flash
as the pennies fall
from the slot
Yankee made
pedalling machine.

A Packet Given to a Child

See,
if you blow hard,
the seed will scatter on that star.
And, if you wait,
will settle and make a star green
in the sky.
Green against black,
white glowing edges.

Some of the seed will land on the earth.
Look, can you see it land?
Blow hard now, blow,
blow, make it grow.

Naming a Child

A relation of mine once beat the metal dry,
made iron burn water snake from the job at hand.

It came to me the other day
walking by a burn, peat red,
old blood,
water ashes, grey years gone.

Fruit tree in a wire cage, inscribed
barren.
Planted to the memory of a person burned.
I did read the inscription
but do not ask me to repeat it.
Forged embarrassment, I suppose.

Cancer white iron bars worked his veins,
cancer white
from the decorator's colour chart,
chosen for the ceiling, for the evening.

After threading chains of red, green and gold,
menopause colours,
during the working day;
after dashing the chains in front of a hot fire,
he would make a snake plum tree
and plant it free, single
and barren it would become.

Seventeen years before the burning,
when you became a memory
and bore fruit.
My grandmother's father
resting by a cancer matt wall
whom no one will visit, no one will write to.

Water Rushes into Veins

Water rushes into veins
madly circulating in no direction
because capillaries force it to.
Alters and re-alters and changes
to come back from no direction.
I feel all at sea, sucked down,
washed, and the empty dry
of distance seen across
to you, half turned, to face the fire
and me to drown.

Depression 1

I no longer hear the cry blue throated birds sing
at speed.
I cannot understand.
Exotic fish roar in the aquarium.
I walk over magic stars.
I cannot understand.
The verse is blank.
Every word is a big word,
you are idiomatic to me.

Depression 2

I no
longer hear bird song
Words are spoken at a speed I
cannot understand
Fish roar in the aquarium

Christianity

The blood of Christ. Twelve pints full,
taken in the sacrament.
The body of the Lord, four bags full
taking in the communion.

Vomit in a bog.

After the Abortion

Max Factor faced, nailed compulsory red.
Starched head and New York suit,
streaked blowhair.
Reversed person-to-person charged call
care of the U S of A., OK?
Charcoal coked eyes care of Medicare Inc.
Limited pay out, paid off.

Vacuum clean the apartment,
tidy the specks, dust the sheets.
Launder the thoughts and remake the face.
Oh yes, and have the abortion.
Then it's Rock and Mary for barbeque at six
and fresh diapers for junior.

The First Day of December

It is first thing, peach light rise,
a salmon turns toward the sun,
December rise,
leaps to the sun,
stretches as high as the dry, grey, stane lain wall
where the overhanging peach tree spreads.

Then down,
back
to November gravel, under water deep
November grey.

It is the first day of December
and your face is as open as the land.

Rings

She had been cleaning,
in the sun, the ring worn
around her wrist; cleaned
since her twenty first year.

Next, she cleaned the ring
worn around her finger,
cleaned since her twenty fifth year.
Polished clean, she said,
by me.

I went out to Christ's-set-
world-wilderness (or what,
today, I thought it might seem).

To scramble alone.
Living a parable, or in a
parable.

Scrambling sand dunes,
I and the sand stood
waiting the sand-night-sky.
I saw polished rings everywhere
in that sky.

None were for me.

Running Without Reason

running without reason

salt wind in my hair
salt tears on your face

rain RAB red tears

marbled whites elusive blues
green man chalk man

Imran

ring fort
will you carry a torch for me
my love?

Free Climb

Free climb.
Masturbate into rock cervix.
ms -1
Two thousand feet fall.
No rope.

Loosely, speed.
Free fall, into an old woman's belly.

I Remember You

I remember you.
When I saw you I was a schoolboy,
you stretched the muscles in my neck.
You turned my head
like a racer for the line.
Eager.
Like the cooper's smack on the iron band
covering the oak cask
with fire inside.

When it came to it
I retreated inside my igloo.

Geometry

Dodging into and jumping out of laid corners,
square,
is not how I move
into corners if they be there.
Into the sudden panic of the square.

Reshape it then, into a valley of response.
Cut the square into a different form . . .
perspective.
Into a channel of bends,
where light has time to bounce
upon the time in the curve.
Shadowing bits of the light, straight
until the dodge is the dark
and the jump the light of the curve,
against the light straight into the curving square.

Trapped

Encased by steel, four sided, with limited drain points.
Encased by movement,
a jig and a jog and that's about it.
Doors, with locks upward and downward
and no keys to turn them.
How do you get out?
You don't,
you sit there, in steel,
waiting for the water to drain.

Sitka Spruce

Bad morning.
Then eleven thirty. Ring.
Then afternoon.

"Please, not to walk there."
"Yes."
"Please, please not there."
It sets off. Head down.
Running at it.
Into the channel.

Sitka spruce. Fire gap.
Into which I am taken.
Uphill. Walking against pressure.
Asbestos and glass fibre wood
stuffed down the throat.
Insulating material. Nostrils choking sitka.
Like a channel into the arse.
Togetherness.

Night.
An all night job.
Love to tears.
Tears that come for the third time in thirty three years.
Count them: 1963, 1969, now.
Before then child's joy, child's sorrow.
Unmistakable.
Crying, tears in full spate.

Forever Gone?

Hands pooled in bowls of lavender
A head shaken, washed by rose snow.

Both once dried by your scent; secretly.
Forever gone?